# CULTURE IN ACTION

# Making a Recording

Liz Miles

**www.raintreepublishers.co.uk**
Visit our website to find out more information about Raintree books.

**To order:**
📞 Phone 0845 6044371
📠 Fax +44 (0) 1865 312263
💻 Email myorders@raintreepublishers.co.uk

Customers from outside the UK please telephone +44 1865 312262

Raintree is an imprint of Capstone Global Library Limited, a company incorporated in England and Wales having its registered office at 7 Pilgrim Street, London, EC4V 6LB – Registered company number: 6695582

Edited by Louise Galpine, Abby Colich, and Laura J. Hensley
Designed by Kimberly Miracle and Betsy Wernert
Original illustrations © Capstone Global Library Ltd 2010
Illustrated by kja-artists.com
Picture research by Mica Brancic and Kay Altwegg
Production by Alison Parsons
Originated by Dot Gradations Ltd
Printed in China by Leo Paper Products

ISBN 978 1 406211 96 2 (hardback)
13 12 11 10 09
10 9 8 7 6 5 4 3 2 1

ISBN 978 1 406212 16 7 (paperback)
14 13 12 11 10
10 9 8 7 6 5 4 3 2 1

**British Library Cataloguing in Publication Data**
Miles, Liz
Making a recording. – (Culture in action)
781.4'9
A full catalogue record for this book is available from the British Library.

**Acknowledgements**
We would like to thank the following for permission to reproduce photographs: Alamy pp. **5** (© J.R. Bale), **14** (Thinkstock/© JupiterImages), **15** (© Dex Image), **16** (© Teenagers), **20** (© Russell Blake), **22** (© The Photolibrary Wales), **24** (Thinkstock/© JupiterImages), **25** (© Everynight Images/Debbie Bragg); Corbis p. **18** (© Radius Images); ©Curtis, Inc. p. **13**; ©esession.com p. **26**; Getty Images pp. **4** (for Pepsi), **8** (Hulton Archive), **9** (Hulton Archive/Robert Whitaker), **12** (Robert Harding World Imagery/Gavin Hellier), **22** (Simone Joyner), **28** (Michael Ochs Archives/Colin Escott), **29 top** (Kevin Winter); Redferns pp. **10** (GAB Archives), **19** (Ebet Roberts), **29 bottom** (Erica Echenberg); Science & Society pp. **6** (Science Museum), **11** (Science Museum); Shutterstock p. **17** (© Andi Hazelwood).

Icon and banner images supplied by Shutterstock: © Alexander Lukin, © ornitopter, © Colourlife, and © David S. Rose.

Cover photograph of a music producer adjusting sound equipment reproduced with permission of Masterfile Royalty Free.

We would like to thank Nancy Harris, Jackie Murphy, and Jon Brennan for their invaluable help in the preparation of this book.

Every effort has been made to contact copyright holders of any material reproduced in this book. Any omissions will be rectified in subsequent printings if notice is given to the publisher.

# Contents

What is recording?     4

Recording history     6

At the recording studio     12

Mixing and mastering     18

Recording outside the studio     22

Famous record producers     28

Glossary     30

Find out more     31

Index     32

Some words are printed in bold, **like this**. You can find out what they mean by looking in the glossary on page 30.

# What is recording?

When you hear your favourite song, you probably do not realise all the time, hard work, and people needed to record it. **Professional** musicians record their music so they can sell copies of it for other people to hear.

How do you and your family listen to music? Recordings come in many forms, such as records, **cassettes**, CDs, and computer files.

Pop stars such as Beyoncé can earn millions from recordings of their music.

## Recording technology

Recording music is a **technology** that has improved over time. Technology is the use of tools, objects, and power to make something work. Today, computers are important tools in recording studios. Big companies use expensive recording equipment. These companies make money by making recordings for films, radio, and television. Listeners want to hear high-quality recordings.

## Billion-pound recordings

The music **industry** is made up of all the people who sell music. The industry makes billions of pounds by selling recorded music. Recordings have made some people very rich and famous. They range from rock stars to **classical** musicians and record **producers**. Record producers control how a piece of music is recorded. Many other people work behind the scenes in recording music. Skilled **technicians** are needed at every stage in recording music. They know how to use all the recording equipment.

## Starting small

Expensive studios are not needed to record music, however. It can be done at home, in small studios, or on location, such as at a live concert. Anyone can make a **demo**. A demo is a recorded example of an artist's work. Demos give unknown musicians the chance to send their music to others. Musicians can record a demo at home, send it to recording companies or managers, and perhaps get a recording **contract**. A contract is a written agreement that will let you create and sell records.

With the right equipment, you can record your own music at home.

# Recording history

In 1877 the first recording of a sound was made. It was made using a machine called a phonograph. Thomas Edison, an inventor, created it. The phonograph stored sound on a cylinder (tube) covered in foil. The cylinder only recorded two to three minutes of sound. This method of recording was unpopular, however, because the cylinders were very expensive to make.

## Gramophone

In 1887 an inventor called Emile Berliner invented a machine called a gramophone. It recorded and played sound on discs called records. To make a record, performers had to sit close to a gramophone horn. This **amplified** the sound (made it louder) so that it could be cut into a groove on a disc (see box at the top of page 7). Using a mould, many copies of each record were made. The new invention meant that one recording could be copied many times.

The invention of the gramophone was a major step in the history of recording.

## How a record works

To make a record, a cutting machine makes a spiralling groove in a disc. The width and depth of the groove matches the volume and **pitch** (highness or lowness) of the sound. When played, a stylus (needle) runs along the groove and picks up the sounds. The sound is then amplified so that it can be heard through speakers.

## Electronic recording

The first electronic recording occurred in 1925. **Microphones** and amplifiers were used. Sound is made of vibrations (back and forth movement) in the air. In electronic recording, a microphone can change these vibrations into **electric current** (flowing electricity). This electric current could then be controlled in ways not previously possible. The volume of each performer could be changed, for example.

## Vinyl records

In 1948 Columbia Records made the first long-playing vinyl (plastic) record. The quality of the sound was better than that of gramophone records. Vinyl records also stored more songs. There are several types of record (see box below).

## Different record types

| RECORD SIZE (IN INCHES) | RECORD TYPE | NUMBER OF SONGS | RECORD SPEED (RPM, OR REVOLUTIONS PER MINUTE) |
| --- | --- | --- | --- |
| 7 | Single | 2 | 45 |
| 10 | EP (extended play) | 4–6 | 78, later 33.3 |
| 12 | Album or LP (long play) | 9–12 | 33.3 |

In the 1950s, early rock-and-roll artists like Elvis Presley made two-track recordings of their music.

## Magnetic tape

The chance to improve recordings became possible with the use of magnetic tape in the late 1940s. When music is recorded on magnetic tape, it is possible to cut out parts of a recorded magnetic tape and insert other parts. This cutting and recombining of different parts is called **editing**. For example, if a singer hits a bad note, that section of a song can be cut and re-recorded. Then a new section of tape can be stuck in. This was a huge development in making recordings. A single performance no longer had to be perfect.

## Two-track recording

Recordings were improved by another development in the 1940s called **multitrack recording**. This meant that two recordings could be put side by side on a single tape, which is known as two **track**. (A track is a single recorded piece of music.) Running side by side, the two recordings played at the same time. By the 1950s, recording artists regularly used two-track recording.

## Stereo sound

In 1958 the first **stereo** records and players went on sale. When previous recordings were played, the sound came out of one speaker. But stereo music comes out of two speakers. There is one track for each speaker. This makes stereo music sound more realistic, since we hear from different directions through our two ears. Stereo music sounds more as if musicians are playing live in a room.

## More tracks

Over time, multiple tracks began to be used. Recordings of different instruments are made at different times. Each track is then edited and adjusted for volume. All the tracks are then **mixed** (combined) into a final recording, from which copies are made. At first, in the early 1960s, recordings were made with four tracks. Over time, **professional** studios learned how to add more and more tracks, for a richer sound.

In 1963 Abbey Road Studios switched from a two-track to a four-track recording system to record the Beatles.

## Cassette tapes

Beginning in the 1970s, **cassette** tapes became a popular way to listen to music. Magnetic tape had been used in recording studios since the 1940s (see page 8). Now it was used in a format that everyone could use. Small, portable plastic cassette cases held two spools of magnetic tape. Each "side" of a cassette tape had two stereo tracks. Tape-playing machines moved the magnetic tape around the spools and produced music. Most home stereos had tape players.

## Digital revolution

In the 1980s, there was a revolution in the recording **industry**: **digital** technology. Digital technology uses computers. Recording, editing, and mixing can all be done on a computer. This is much easier than cutting tape. People also do not need expensive, bulky equipment. They can record anywhere, even at home.

Digital technology introduced new ways for people to listen to music. In 1982 the first digital compact disc (CD) was introduced in Japan. The sound on a CD is very clear compared to records and cassettes. At first, CD players were expensive. But as the technology became more affordable, CDs went on to become very popular.

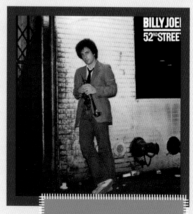

In 1982 the first CD was released. It was a recording of singer-songwriter Billy Joel's music.

Over time, digital technology expanded to include mini discs, digital audiotapes, MP3s, DVDs, and Blu-ray discs. In the 2000s, the increasing popularity of digital downloads began to hurt the sales of CDs. New technology will continue to develop and change the way people record and listen to music.

# Design your own label

Imagine you own a record company. Think of a name for your company and design a **logo** for your vinyl records. A company's logo is a design that is easy to remember. It often includes the company name and a picture.

The logo for a record company called "His Master's Voice" included a dog and gramophone, as seen on this gramophone label.

## Steps to follow:

1. With the help of an adult, research record logos on the Internet, for example, Warner Bros or Columbia Records.

2. Decide what sort of music you want your own record company to record: **classical**, jazz, rock, hip-hop, or something else? Think of a record company name that would suit this kind of music.

3. Visualise your logo. This might just be the name in a certain pattern. Or you may want a small picture that you think would make it stand out.

4. Sketch your label name and logo. Try different designs and colours. Redesign until you like it.

5. When you are happy with the design of your company name and logo, create a final copy.

## Remember that the design should:

- fit neatly in the circular label
- suit the style of music
- stand out and be memorable.

# At the recording studio

Recording music involves a team of skilled people and advanced **technology**. It usually takes place in a special building called a recording studio.

## The studio

Some recording studios are big enough to fit in a full orchestra. Some only record **soloists** (artists who perform alone) or small bands.

Studios are soundproof. This means that noise from outside, such as the siren of a fire engine, will not be heard in a recording studio.

Studios are also designed so that the **acoustics** are controlled. Acoustics are the way sound behaves in different places. For example, in a thickly carpeted room, the acoustics would be poor and the sound would be muffled. Studios are built with materials that make the sounds clear and crisp.

Sun Studio in Memphis, USA, is famous for recording Elvis Presley's first hit record in 1953. Presley went on to become a rock legend.

control room

isolation booth

performance area

Recording equipment is kept in a control room. Musicians play music in a separate performance area.

# Parts of a studio

A recording studio has the following areas:

- Performance area: A room where the musician or musicians play music.

- Isolation booth: Small room where especially loud instruments, such as drums, are played. This keeps their sound away from other recording areas. For example, microphones in the performance area will not pick up sounds played in an isolation booth.

- Control room: A room where all the recording and editing equipment is kept. Windows between the rooms allow performers, record **producers**, and other members of the team to see one another.

# The equipment

A large recording studio may hold expensive equipment. This includes **microphones** and **multitrack recording** equipment. Panels with rows of switches and dials are used to control the recording, **editing**, and **mixing** of the music.

# Record producer

A record producer, also called a music producer, is the boss in a studio. He or she supervises the recording and mixing. Getting the performers to do their best is part of the job.

Record producers are powerful people in the music **industry**. They choose the style of music that goes on sale. They can help make a performer famous.

# Recording engineer

**Engineers** are people who know how to use machines. Recording engineers both record and mix the music. They are skilled **technicians** and sometimes musicians. They must notice the smallest problem. For example, they might notice that a singer makes a *b* in a word sound louder than the rest of a sentence.

Record producers oversee every part of the recording process.

# Mastering engineer

When the recording engineer is happy with a recording, it is given to a **mastering** engineer. The mastering engineer does a final mix and puts the recording onto a CD or other storage device (called the master). This is the last stage before the music is copied and sold. (For more about mastering, see page 20.)

## How to be a recording engineer

To take on the job of a recording engineer, you need to love music as well as electronic equipment. Recording engineers have often studied engineering, electronics, or radio and television. Even then, a first job in a studio might be as a "runner" or "studio intern". People in these jobs take care of musicians and technicians by making sure they have everything they need.

An assistant learns a lot about recording music while working in a studio.

## Recording sessions

Recordings are made during periods of time called **sessions**. During a recording session, an artist sings or plays in the soundproof performance area, or booth. The recording engineer records music in several parts, called **takes**. Each take is recorded separately. There may be several takes of one performer. For example, the producer might ask a singer to do another take and sing more softly.

## Drums first

When recording rock music, **percussion** instruments, such as drums, are usually recorded first. The drums set the **rhythm** (regular beat). The other musicians play using that rhythm. They can listen to it quietly on earphones when it is their turn to be recorded. Other instruments are recorded next, such as guitars. The last section to be recorded is the vocals. Singers adjust their voice to suit the tempo (speed) and the volume of the music that has already been recorded.

Loud drums are recorded in an isolation booth.

# Red-light fever

Some performers get nervous in front of the microphone and an audience of **professionals**. They are said to be suffering from "red-light fever".

A red light tells everyone that recording is in progress.

## Adjusting sounds

Throughout each recording session, the recording engineer is focused on capturing the best sound from each instrument. Microphones might be changed and levels of sound changed. For example, levels for lower-**pitched** instruments, such as the bass guitar, might be increased.

## Multitracking in the studio

**Multitracking** means recording vocals and instruments separately. Different sections of a piece of music can be recorded separately, too, such as a guitar solo. All the separate pieces are adjusted and then put together to complete a song.

Multitrack recording is used to record rock bands and singers. **Classical** music is usually recorded with a whole orchestra playing at the same time. Classical music is a type of music written between 1750 and 1830, or music that is more lasting than pop music.

# Mixing and mastering

An **engineer** known as a mixer takes over after the recording **sessions** are finished. A mixer combines all the separate **tracks**. The goal is for each instrument to be heard clearly when they are all **mixed** together. Mixing equipment is used to make hundreds, or thousands, of changes.

## What is a remix?

**Multitrack recordings** are sometimes kept and remixed again later. The music is sold as a "remix".

A mixing engineer changes the quality of sounds using buttons, sliders, and switches.

# Mixing effects

Some of the **effects** mixers can use include:

- Equalization: The mixer can change the sound of instruments or singers. The mixer can increase (boost) or reduce (cut) the **pitch** of sounds. For example, the lower-pitch sounds of a bass guitar could be reduced.

- Reverb: This makes recorded music sound like it is being played in a certain type of room. It can change the music so it sounds as if it is being played in a small cave or a large church, for example.

- Delay: This effect is when notes are played back several times. A whole set of notes can be repeated. This is called a loop. The delay effect can sound like an echo.

Once the mixing is finished, the recording is usually in the form of two tracks – one for each **stereo** speaker. It is ready for the final stage: **mastering**.

Bobby McFerrin uses just his own voice to record songs that have several vocal and percussion parts.

## Bobby McFerrin

US performer Bobby McFerrin can imitate **percussion** instruments with his voice and by tapping his chest. Multitrack recordings of his voice and the percussion sounds are mixed to make music that sounds like several voices and percussion instruments playing together.

Mastering is done in a different studio from where the recording is done.

## Mastering

When the final mix is complete, the music is given to a mastering engineer. This skilled engineer puts the final mix on a storage device. It is not just a matter of copying it. A lot of changes still have to be made. The performer might be involved at this stage, too. That way, when the finished recording goes on sale, it will sound exactly like he or she hoped.

Any fade-ins or fade-outs are done at this stage. For example, some tracks may fade out, meaning the sound slowly fades away, rather than coming to a sudden end. The gaps of silence between different songs are finished at this stage, too.

## Buying music

The finished recording is copied to CDs. Labels and covers are designed and printed. Recorded music is also put on websites on the Internet. People can pay to copy the music to their computer or portable media player. Check with your teacher or parent before you download music from the Internet. Most music has to be paid for.

## MUSIC ACTIVITY

# The final mix

By listening closely to recorded music, you will gain some important skills. Careful listening can help you to record your own or others' music.

## Steps to follow:

1. Listen to a favourite song. How many different musical parts can you hear? Write down the different instruments and singers you can hear. These may each have been recorded on a different track. Share your ideas with a friend.

2. Listen for any special effects. Perhaps you can hear some of the following:

   - Are some instruments louder and then softer?
   - Are some notes or sequences repeated?
   - Can you hear any echoes?
   - Are there any fade-ins or fade-outs?

3. Imagine you are doing a remix of the track. What would you change?

4. Repeat the steps above using other songs.

# Recording outside the studio

Musical performances are often recorded outside **professional** studios. Some live music is recorded "on location", such as in concert halls.

## On location

For recordings on location, recording **engineers** must take their equipment to the location where the recording is taking place. This could include **microphones**, cables (thick wires), a portable mixer, and recording equipment.

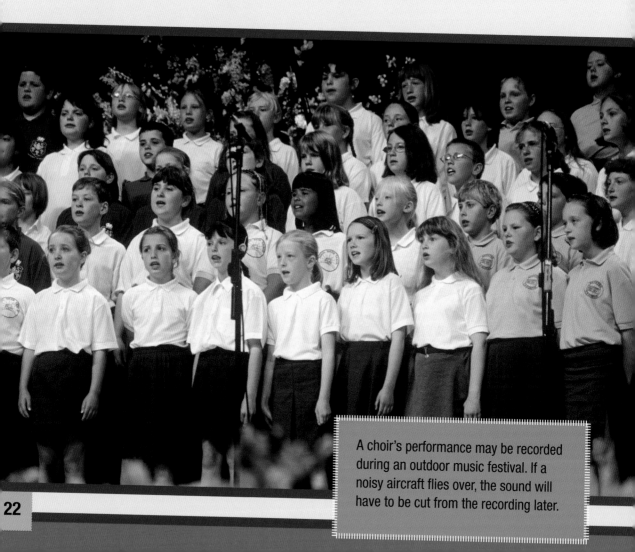

A choir's performance may be recorded during an outdoor music festival. If a noisy aircraft flies over, the sound will have to be cut from the recording later.

Everything has to be set up to work with the type of singers and the instruments being played. **Technicians** need to think about where the performers will be standing or sitting. The **acoustics** of the venue (the way sound behaves there) will also affect the work of engineers.

A near-final mix has to be made at the location where the recording takes place. There will not be another opportunity for a new **take**.

On-location recording can be challenging. For example, while recording a school orchestra, musicians might bump into their music stands, or instruments might drown out the choir. **Editing** and **mixing** will later fix these problems.

# Live recordings

There is only one opportunity to record a live performance. Lots of equipment is needed to make a recording of an event or concert. At a large concert with many bands, there is a large team of technicians. During rehearsals, the technicians must set up their equipment. At that time, microphones are put into place and sound levels are checked.

In a live recording, the sound of an excited audience must not drown out the music itself.

# Home recordings

Many people do their own recordings at home. A home studio could be a **producer's** or musician's home studio (often specially built). It could be a corner in a bedroom. The sound will not be as good as in professionally built studios. But recording at home means people can record themselves or others as a hobby.

If you set up your own recording studio at home, do not forget soundproofing. It helps not to have outdoor sounds coming in. And it also helps not to annoy neighbours with loud instruments! Closed doors and windows are a good start.

The simplest studio needs some basic equipment to record, re-record, edit, and mix the sounds. The easiest and cheapest way to do a home recording is to try **multitrack recording**. Multitrack recording equipment can record four or more **tracks**. You can then blend or mix together. You will also need a microphone and at least one musician – who could be yourself, of course!

With the right equipment, you can set up your own recording studio at home.

# Computer recordings

Most computers can be used to record and mix music. In addition to the computer, you will need:

- a sound card (which lets you move music into and out of your computer)

- computer **software** (programs) for recording and editing music or other sounds

- a microphone

- a musical keyboard (although not necessary, this is also useful).

Free recording software is available on the Internet. For example, a software program called Audacity lets you record, edit, and play sounds.

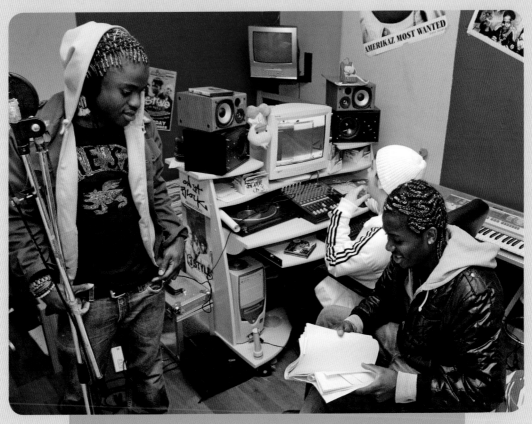

This band is making a recording of their music using a computer.

Musicians can send their recorded music to an online studio. They can ask to have guitar, bass, and drum music added.

# Online recording

Online recording lets musicians record music nearly anywhere, as long as they have the right equipment. Composers, musicians, and recording studios sometimes get together over the Internet to record music online. Music can be sent over the Internet to a studio. There, engineers add extra parts, such as the drum tracks. Online studios can also mix and **master** music. They can also supply an extra track for people to mix with their own recordings at home.

# Posting demos online

Musicians who are just starting out make **demos** to show off their music. Musicians can put their demos on special websites on the Internet. They hope that a producer will listen to it and like it enough to offer them a **contract**.

# Make a demo

Do you think you could be a record producer, studio technician, or performer?

**You will need:**

- an audio recorder, such as a **cassette** recorder or a computer

- a microphone (a cassette recorder or computer may have a built-in microphone)

- a musical instrument (this can be your singing voice).

**Steps to follow:**

**1.** Decide on a piece of music to play.

**2.** Practise it until you are happy with the sound.

**3.** Set up your recording equipment and record your performance.

**4.** Listen to the recording and re-record until you are happy with it. Things to think about are:

- Is the microphone too close or too far away?

- Do you need to play/sing some parts slower or faster?

- Do you need to play/sing some parts louder or quieter?

**5.** Re-record until you are happy with the result.

# Famous record producers

A lot of people have made their name as record **producers**. They have brought new ideas to the world of recording music. Here are just a few of them.

## Les Paul (born 1915)

Les Paul is a US jazz guitarist who invented a lot of recording tools and **effects** (sounds that make the impression of something, such as an echo). The famous singer Bing Crosby gave Paul a tape recorder. Paul used the machine to record two **tracks** alongside each other. In doing this, he invented **multitrack recording**.

## Sam Phillips (1923–2003)

US record producer Sam Phillips brought about the rise of rock-and-roll music. He is especially famous for discovering Elvis Presley. Phillips aimed to get feeling into the music he recorded.

## Phil Spector (born 1940)

In the early 1960s, US record producer Phil Spector came up with a recording technique called the "Wall of Sound". It gave pop music a new, layered sound.

Sam Phillips' record label, Sun Records, made musicians famous.

## Eddie Kramer (born 1941)

Born in South Africa, the legendary recording **engineer** and producer Eddie Kramer worked with many musicians. In 1969 he recorded one of the first big music festivals, Woodstock (in New York). He became known as the most important producer of live music recordings.

## Judith Sherman (born 1942)

US record producer Judith Sherman started her career as an engineer. She is now an award-winning **classical** music producer. She has worked closely with many successful composers, such as Philip Glass.

Judith Sherman has won many awards for her work.

## Brian Eno (born 1948)

Although a successful musician, Englishman Brian Eno is best known as a record producer, working with musicians such as Talking Heads and David Bowie. He was the first to use the phrase *ambient music* – a type of music that is soft and electronic.

Brian Eno was in a rock band called Roxy Music before he became a producer.

## Trevor Horn (born 1949)

English record producer Trevor Horn became well known in the 1980s, working with performers such as Art of Noise, Seal, and Pet Shop Boys. He was one of the first producers to use computers successfully in recording music.

## Trina Shoemaker (born 1965)

Trina Shoemaker is a US mixer, record producer, and sound engineer. She has worked with stars such as Iggy Pop, Sheryl Crow, and Nanci Griffith. She has won major music awards for her recording skills.

# Glossary

**acoustics** way sound behaves in different places. The acoustics in a carpet-lined room would be poor and the sound would be muffled.

**amplify** make louder. An amplifier is a machine that makes sounds louder.

**cassette** tape in a plastic case that runs from spindle to spindle. Compact cassettes are small and were popular before the invention of compact discs (CDs).

**classical** type of music written between 1750 and 1830, or music that is more lasting than pop music

**contract** written agreement. A recording contract says what the musician and the recording company have agreed upon, such as when a record will be made.

**demo** demonstration, or example, of a musician's work. A demo is sometimes recorded using simple equipment at home.

**digital** special kind of electronic signals that computers use to store and change information. The sound on CDs is stored in a digital form.

**edit** cut and stick together different parts to improve the whole. Noise from an audience can be edited out of a recording of a live performance.

**effect** in music, a sound meant to create the impression of something, such as an echo

**electric current** flowing electricity

**engineer** someone who makes or uses machines. A recording engineer uses recording and mixing machines.

**industry** all the companies or groups of people who make and sell something. The music industry makes, records, and sells music.

**logo** design that is used to represent a company. A logo often includes a company name and a picture.

**master** create a finished recording. The word is also used to describe the finished recording itself.

**microphone** machine that picks up sounds and changes them into electrical signals

**mix** combine a number of tracks to make one sound. Sounds are altered and effects are added during the mixing process.

**multitrack recording** process of recording in which different parts, such as instruments, are recorded separately

**multitracking** recording vocals and instruments separately

**percussion** type of musical instrument, such as a drum, that is struck or shaken to make sound

**pitch** how high or low a sound is

**producer** in music, the person who controls how a piece of music is recorded and who also guides the performers

**professional** person who is paid for his or her work

**rhythm** regular beat

**session** time spent doing one thing. A recording session is a length of time, such as a day, spent recording music.

**software** computer program

**soloist** artist who performs alone

**stereo** short for *stereophonic*, it is music made up of two parts

**take** individual piece of recorded music

**technician** person who knows how to use and fix machines

**technology** use of tools, objects, and power to make things work

**track** one recorded song or piece of music

# Find out more

## Books

*Career Ideas for Kids Who Like Music and Dance*, Diane Lindsey Reeves and Lindsey Clasen (Facts on File Inc, 2007)

*How Does It Work?: Music Technology*, John Hilvert, Linda Bruce, and Alan Hilvert-Bruce (Nelson Thornes, 2008)

*People at Work: Creative and Media*, Jan Champney (Franklin Watts, 2008)

*So You Want to Work in Music and Dance?*, Margaret McAlpine (Wayland, 2005)

## Websites

Kids rock
www.kidsrock.org

Music professions
http://library.thinkquest.org/15413/professions/professions.htm

## Visit a recording studio

There are a number of recording studios around the country where you can go to record a song with the help of experienced technicians. Use a children's search engine on the Internet, such as Ask Kids, to find more information.

# Index

Abbey Road Studios 9
acoustics 12, 23
amplification 6, 7

Beatles 9
Berliner, Emile 6
Blu-ray discs 10

cassettes 4, 10, 27
CDs 4, 10, 15, 20
classical music 4, 17
computer recordings 4, 10, 25
computer software 25
contracts 5, 26

delay 19
demos 5, 26, 27
digital audiotapes 10
digital technology 10
drums 13, 16, 26
DVDs 10

Edison, Thomas 6
editing 8, 13, 23, 25
electric current 7
electronic recording 7
equalization 19
equipment 4, 13, 18, 22, 23,
    24, 25, 27

fade-ins and fade-outs 20

gramophone records 6, 7, 11
gramophones 6

history of recording 6–10
home recordings 5, 24–25

Internet
    downloading music from 10,
    20
    online recording 10, 26
    posting demos online 26

isolation booths 13, 16

logos 11
loops 19

McFerrin, Bobby 19
magnetic tape 8, 10
mastering 15, 19, 20, 26
mastering engineers 15, 20
microphones 7, 13, 17, 22, 23,
    24, 25, 27
mini discs 10
mixing 9, 13, 14, 15, 18–19,
    23, 26
    delay 19
    equalization 19
    reverb 19
mixing engineers 18
MP3s 10
multitrack recordings 8, 9, 13,
    17, 18, 19, 24, 28
music industry 4, 14
musical keyboards 25

on-location recording 5,
    22–23
online recording 26

percussion instruments 16, 19
phonographs 6
pitch 7, 17, 19
pop stars 4
Presley, Elvis 8, 12, 28

record producers 4, 13, 14,
    28–29
recording engineers 14, 15,
    16, 17, 22
recording sessions 8–9,
    16–17, 18

recording studios 5, 9, 12–20,
    26
    acoustics 12
    control room 13
    equipment 13, 18
    home studios 24
    isolation booths 13, 16
    online studios 26
    performance area 13, 16
    soundproofing 12, 24
    technicians 14–15, 16, 17,
    18, 20
records 4
    gramophone records 6, 7,
    11
    logos 11
    making a record 7
    vinyl records 7, 11
red-light fever 17
remixes 18, 21
reverb 19
rock music 16, 17
runners 15

soloists 12
sound cards 25
soundproofing 12, 24
speakers 7, 9, 19
stereo sound 8, 9
studio interns 15
stylus 7
Sun Studio 12

takes 16, 23
technicians 4, 14–15, 17, 18,
    20, 22, 23
tracks 8, 18, 19, 20, 24, 26

vibrations 7
vinyl records 7, 11

"Wall of Sound" 28